D0949915

Praise for
One Word That Will Change Your Life

"*One Word* is a great little book that conveys a profoundly simple idea. Discover your *One ~~Wo~~rd* for the year, own it, live it, and experi- ~~ence~~ its impact on your life. One word for this ~~book?~~ Priceless!"

—**Ken Blanchard,** coauthor of
The One Minute Manager® and
Leading at a Higher Level

~~d~~
~~n~~
~~most~~

~~President~~ of
~~Coach~~ Inc.

~~whe~~n feel cluttered, confused,
~~One W~~*ord* shows the way to
It guides you to what
~~matters~~ most and clarifies how
~~One Word~~ is a game-changing
~~h   h~~ow you do your
~~One W~~*ord*. Find your
~~experie~~nce the best

Authentic
~~Le~~adership, Inc.

"In the past 10 years, I've been asked to editorially review at least 1,000 books on leadership, personal change, and life purpose. If I were forced to choose one favorite among them, my number one choice would be *One Word That Will Change Your Life*. Why? In a word, the book makes a bold promise—and then it delivers. I've read it cover to cover twice now. Dan, Jimmy, and Jon have produced a gift that will do just what it says: change your life! I recommend you embark on the thrilling One Word adventure an invite your friends, family, and coworkers to jo you. I predict you'll soon have some of your interesting experiences ever."

—**Ron Forseth,** Vice Presi
Business Development, Outre

One Word

One Word

that
will change
your life

DAN BRITTON JIMMY PAGE JON GORDON

WILEY

John Wiley & Sons, Inc.

Cover image and design: Michael J. Freeland

Copyright © 2013 by Dan Britton, Jimmy Page, and Jon Gordon. All rights reserved.

Published by John Wiley & Sons, Inc., Hoboken, New Jersey.
Published simultaneously in Canada.

No part of this publication may be reproduced, stored in a retrieval system, or transmitted in any form or by any means, electronic, mechanical, photocopying, recording, scanning, or otherwise, except as permitted under Section 107 or 108 of the 1976 United States Copyright Act, without either the prior written permission of the Publisher, or authorization through payment of the appropriate per-copy fee to the Copyright Clearance Center, 222 Rosewood Drive, Danvers, MA 01923, (978) 750-8400, fax (978) 646-8600, or on the web at www.copyright.com. Requests to the Publisher for permission should be addressed to the Permissions Department, John Wiley & Sons, Inc., 111 River Street, Hoboken, NJ 07030, (201) 748-6011, fax (201) 748-6008, or online at www.wiley.com/go/permissions.

Limit of Liability/Disclaimer of Warranty: While the publisher and author have used their best efforts in preparing this book, they make no representations or warranties with the respect to the accuracy or completeness of the contents of this book and specifically disclaim any implied warranties of merchantability or fitness for a particular purpose. No warranty may be created or extended by sales representatives or written sales materials. The advice and strategies contained herein may not be suitable for your situation. You should consult with a professional where appropriate. Neither the publisher nor the author shall be liable for damages arising herefrom.

For general information about our other products and services, please contact our Customer Care Department within the United States at (800) 762-2974, outside the United States at (317) 572-3993 or fax (317) 572-4002.

Wiley publishes in a variety of print and electronic formats and by print-on-demand. Some material included with standard print versions of this book may not be included in e-books or in print-on-demand. If this book refers to media such as a CD or DVD that is not included in the version you purchased, you may download this material at http://booksupport.wiley.com. For more information about Wiley products, visit www.wiley.com.

ISBN 978-1-118-54241-5 (cloth); ISBN 978-1-118-54890-5 (ebk);
ISBN 978-1-118-54889-9 (ebk); ISBN 978-1-118-54895-0 (ebk)

Printed in the United States of America

10 9 8 7 6 5

If you want your life to change . . .
to be more rewarding and exciting than ever . . .
you can do it with just **_One Word_**.
We guarantee it.

contents

Introduction

If we could give you one thing that would improve your life in incredible ways, would you receive it? *If* this one thing was so intuitive and easy to use that you would be crazy not to try it—would you give it a shot?

What is this one thing? It's just *One Word*. That's right—*One Word That Will Change Your Life.*

In this book we will show you how to discover the word that is meant for you. It's your *One Word* vision or theme for the entire year, and it will help you become the person you were born to be.

When we first discovered this simple concept in 1999, we never imagined thousands of people would experience life change year after year. However, over the years we have witnessed others experiencing the same life change we have experienced. We came to realize that we had to share this life-changing concept with as many people as possible.

A simple concept must be communicated in a simple way. That's why we have designed this book so that you can read it in just 44 minutes. In this case, less is best. Simple is powerful.

One Word That Will Change Your Life is a proven way to create clarity, power, passion, and life change. Each year, resolutions are rarely kept and goals are often easily forgotten. But *One Word* sticks. By living a single word that is meant for you, you'll find renewed purpose and meaning throughout the year and laserlike focus and power for your life.

We have created a *One Word* process that has three steps:

1. *Prepare Your Heart.* This is where you take action to strategically disengage from the hectic pace of life and look inside. Eliminating noise and clutter properly prepares you for the work of the heart. We show you easy, practical ways to create some space and get ready for your *One Word*.
2. *Discover Your Word.* This step helps you ask simple questions to find your word.

We believe that there is a word meant just for you, and we guide you on the pathway to discover it. You will learn the four key questions to ask that will reveal your word.

3. *Live Your Word.* This is the fun part. We help you experience your word and apply it to every area of life. This step will inspire you along the journey as you live your word with purpose and passion every day throughout the year.

We have also created an action plan featured at the end of the book to help you implement and apply the *One Word* process and live your word for the year.

To maximize your *One Word* experience, we invite you to visit www.GetOneWord.com, where you can receive additional insights, read stories of impact, and download helpful resources.

Join thousands of people and hundreds of schools, businesses, churches, and sports teams who have found their word . . . and discover how to harness the transformational power of *your One Word*. Let's get started and enjoy the journey together!

balance
purpose
commitment
GO LOVE
opportunity
give ask
thankful
generous

the story of *One Word*

Every New Year, 87 percent of adults—more than 206 million people—create new goals and resolutions, only to experience the same frustrating results: false starts and failure. In fact, 50 percent of resolution makers will fail by the end of January! You read that right. Only half of us stick to our convictions for even 30 days. Most resolutions are long forgotten by summer. We derail and give up. That's why an endless number of books and articles are written each year promising a "new you" and "your best life now."

87 percent of us make New Year's resolutions every year!

While these resolutions are meant to be good and well-intentioned solutions, unfortunately they are built on a flawed foundation of more effort, willpower, and goal setting. We set "to do" goals instead of "to be" goals. Success is measured by what we accomplish instead of who we become. Making resolutions convinces us that all we have to do is roll up our sleeves again and get to work. The practice encourages us to put the power of life change in our *heads and hands* with a game plan to change *our habits* and then turns us loose. This approach ignores the most important part of life change—*the heart.*

We have also done our fair share of goal setting and resolution making at the start of each New Year, only to experience the same frustrating outcome. You know the routine. Try and fail; move forward and fall backward. Our hope was to get better by setting goals and making resolutions, but we always came up short.

The most important part of life change is a change of the heart.

We felt the sting of failure, followed by frustration and guilt. Whether we wanted to effect change in our marriage, our health, our workplace, or our finances, we agreed that we wanted things to be different. Yet we were also living the definition of *insanity*: doing the same things over and over again and expecting different results. We've all heard the saying, "If you do what you've always done, you'll get what you always got." Time and time again, our best intentions crashed and burned.

Something Needed to Change

In 1999 we discovered the solution to failed resolutions and unrealized goals. Instead of trying to develop more willpower, we found a simple way to live more powerfully. Instead of creating goals and resolutions, we found a single word that would be our driving force for the year. No goals. No resolutions. Just *One Word*! We simply developed a *One Word* theme for the year. It became a *One Word* vision for everything, and it changed our lives.

We decided to try a radical new approach to the New Year!

By simplifying our approach, we discovered the secret to life change. Our formula is not rooted in our strength and resolve, but in surrender and simplicity. It is not based on temporary inspiration or on the latest pep talk. It's found in narrowing our focus, because we believe less is best. For us, simplicity created clarity, power, and passion.

Some of you are probably thinking, *"One Word?"* That's right, *just a single word*. Not a phrase, not a statement, not a list—just a single word.

Our initial desire was to create a well-crafted mission statement or cool slogan, because something inside us always wants to make things more complicated than they need to be. But the truth is, people do not remember paragraphs or even sentences. Such complexity leads to procrastination and even paralysis. *One Word* is sticky and memorable. We've never forgotten our word!

We've learned firsthand that the secret to a simplified life is *One Word*. Words like *Serving, Purpose, Grace, Surrender, Power,* and *Discipline* have shaped and molded us in amazing ways. By embracing, owning, and living a single word for 365 days, our lives changed. Instead of being weighed down with unrealistic resolutions and unmet goals, *One Word* provides a whole new perspective on how we approach our year. It frees us up. *One Word* gives us renewed purpose and meaning.

One Word creates laserlike focus that lasts.

For us, this *One Word* process has created laser-like focus throughout the year. It has become a driving force and stretches us in all six dimensions of life—spiritually, physically, mentally, relationally, emotionally, and financially. We've been transformed in many ways through this process, and we promise you'll experience transformation, too.

Our Stories

Everyone has his or her own story of experiencing the *One Word* process and the impact it makes. We'd like to share our stories with you.

Dan's Story

In 1999, my friend Steve Fitzhugh and I were traveling to Ocean City, Maryland, to speak at a large youth conference. On this cold December drive, Steve asked me what my theme would be for the upcoming year. After taking several minutes to think about all that I wanted to accomplish, I responded with all my hopes and dreams for the New Year. He listened patiently as I shared an inspiring speech of all the significant changes that would take place.

Steve responded, "That's great, Dan, but I asked for one word, not a sermon."

After considerably more contemplation, I responded with my slogan: "Live it out."

Steve challenged me again, saying, "Dan, that's still not one word."

I grew aggravated with my own inability to sum it up in a single word. It was too difficult to summarize in a single word all of my lofty goals, my massive game plan for the year, and those soon-to-be dramatic life changes.

I told Steve I needed more time to pray and think about it. Several weeks later, I called Steve and told him my word for the year was *Intimacy*, because I desired to have greater intimacy in all areas of my life, including my relationships with my wife, my family, my friends, and God. As a father, husband, friend, leader, and athlete, I was transformed and went to a deeper level in all my relationships. It was the year of *Intimacy.*

Jimmy's Story

From our earliest days as friends, Dan and I pushed each other to be our very best. So when Dan described the idea of narrowing the focus for greater life change, I was all in. I was craving simplicity, but drowning in my endless list of things to improve. Year after year, every single word—from *Go* to *Surrender* to *Power*—has changed me and the direction of my life in remarkable ways.

But the *One Word* that packed the biggest punch came in 2011—*Life.* For such a small word, it had a huge impact!

Personally, I thought it was going to be an easy year, but I couldn't have been more wrong. I quickly discovered that some of the words I spoke to those I loved most were not bringing life, but were critical and demanding. As an encourager, I saw this as an opportunity to get it right. I then discovered that, even though I'm a health nut, some of the food I ate was not bringing me life at all. And when I started to listen to my thoughts, I realized I had some negative, self-defeating patterns of thinking that were preventing me from attempting great things and from living life to the fullest. I then took a look at my relationships and realized I had plenty of opportunities to be giving life to those around me, but that I was missing some. At work, the same was true. It was difficult to face the facts, but it was exhilarating to experience progress in all areas of my life.

Jon's Story

Dan and Jimmy shared the *One Word* concept with me, and I thought it was a brilliant idea.

I passed it on to my wife and kids, and they all came up with their own *One Word* vision.

My word was *Purpose.* I was going to be traveling a ton that year to deliver keynotes around the country, and, over time, airplanes, airports, and grueling schedules can wear me down. However, by focusing on my purpose to make a difference, I knew it would fuel me, replenish me, and keep me going on the road and at home. I knew that if I kept my purpose bigger than my challenges, I would be as energized all year long.

My wife's word was *Intentional.* She realized she wanted to do more things with intention and to be intentional about her life, her decisions, and her health.

My 12-year-old daughter's word was *Drive.* I joked that my wife came up with the word for her, because she needs to spend more time studying than texting friends.

My 10-year-old son came up with the word *Focus.* As soon as I asked him about his word, he said *Focus* without hesitation. He wanted to focus more at school and on the tennis court.

Our *One Words* became a driving force in our lives and family; even my daughter was more motivated than ever. I saw the power *One Word* can have and had to share it with others.

Since that time, I have shared Dan and Jimmy's *One Word* process with countless audiences, companies, schools, and even NFL teams. The feedback has been incredible. And I know first-hand the power *One Word* can have on the lives of all who discover, live, and share their word.

Tap into the Power

Every time we share the *One Word* process, it strikes a chord in our audiences. It's a catalyst for immediate focus and life change . . . one so powerful that we wanted to share it with as many people as possible.

That's why we wrote this book.

the Power of *One Word*

Words are powerful. They have the power to inspire, encourage, appreciate, heal, and turn the impossible into the possible. Throughout history, words have transformed societies, people, and relationships. Words have inspired us to put a man on the moon, advance racial equality, and heal after our greatest tragedies.

But can *One Word* really make a difference? We know that words are powerful when spoken in sentences and when included in inspiring speeches, but can *One Word* on its own really change your life?

One Word can make a difference.

Our answer is an emphatic *yes*. After nearly 15 years of doing this ourselves and taking others through the *One Word* process as part of our workshops, we've found that when you find your word for the year, it will change the way you think, the words you speak, the attitudes of your heart, your relationships, and even your actions.

Similar to buying a new car and suddenly seeing the same model everywhere you go, you'll begin to see your *One Word* everywhere. *One Word* will give you clarity and focus for the challenges of a busy, stress-filled world. Just as a light focused becomes a laser that can cut through steel, a life focused with *One Word* becomes a force that can cut through the status quo. *One Word* is both simple and powerful. Simplicity, done right, will always bring impact.

One Word also creates powerful relationships. When those closest to you know your *One Word*, you can count on them sharpening, challenging, and stretching you to new heights. We often hear encouragement from our loved ones to maximize our word and live it out.

Your Stretch Team will fan the flames of impact.

We encourage you to share it with your inner circle—family and close friends. This group, your *Stretch Team*, will encourage, motivate, and celebrate your success.

People who believe the best in you will fan the flames of impact, because they truly want to make you better.

The Six Dimensions

As *One Word* works its way into every aspect of your life, the concept will powerfully impact the six dimensions mentioned in Chapter 1: spiritual, physical, emotional, relational, mental, and financial. We know, because it happened to us.

Here are examples of how our words have brought transformation in each of the six areas:

1. *Spiritual impact.* Dan's word in 2005 was *Breakthrough.* His desire was to experience *Breakthrough* in every area of his life, especially spiritually. The goal was to go from the ordinary to the extraordinary by identifying specific obstacles and barriers that were keeping him from going to the next level. By removing barriers, his spiritual disciplines were renewed.
2. *Physical impact.* Ivelisse (Jimmy's wife) chose *Believe* for her word in 2008.

Later that year, she was diagnosed with fourth-stage cancer and given very slim odds for survival. She learned the depths and dimensions of her word as she began to trust that God could do the impossible. She learned to believe and trust, no matter what, and received physical healing in the process.

3. *Emotional impact.* In 2012, Jon's word was a choice between *Surrender* and *Enjoy.* When he made his annual New Year's jump into the ocean, he felt a sharp pain in his knee and had trouble walking out of the ocean. *Not a great way to start the year,* he thought. But as he reached the shore he heard the word *Surrender* loud and clear. He was not in control.

4. *Relational impact.* Dan's word in 2008 was *Healing.* His dad was battling leukemia, and Dan was hoping and praying for physical healing. Even though his dad passed away, the healing that took place was relational, as Dan witnessed the touching and healing of hearts from past pain and hurt.

5. *Mental impact*. Jimmy's word in 2007 was *Detox*. He wanted to remove the toxic stuff in his life that was keeping him from being his best. Believing that most challenges in life originate with toxic thinking, Jimmy began to examine his thought life and remove negative, critical patterns of thinking. He replaced those thoughts with positivity, possibility, and faith. This has helped fuel closer relationships and an overcoming spirit.

6. *Financial impact*. In 2011, Jon facilitated the *One Word* process with his company, whereby each employee created his or her own word. The result was more focus, power, energy, and engagement—and the company had its best year ever.

The power of *One Word* is found in its narrow focus and broad impact. Less really turns out to be best. Simple is powerful. *One Word* can really make a difference! Now you just have to find your word.

balance
purpose
contentment
GO LOVE
opportunity
give ask
thankful
generous

balance

purpose

commitment

GO LOVE

opportunity

GIVE ask

thankful

generous

the *One Word* process

In the movie *City Slickers*, Billy Crystal plays Mitch, a vacationing businessman who, along with two friends, takes on the adventure of a cattle drive. In the middle of the drive, a rough-necked cowhand named Curly tells Mitch that the secret to life is just one thing. Curly emphasizes the point by holding up one finger and saying, "You need to stick to that one thing." Mitch asks, "What is that one thing?" Curly responds, "That is what you gotta figure out!"

One thing changes everything.

Now that you understand the history and power of *One Word*, you are probably wondering how you figure out your *One Word*.

Through our own experiences and our work with countless others, we've developed a simple, three-step process that will provide an easy framework for finding your *One Word*:

1. Prepare your heart by looking in.
2. Discover your word by looking up.
3. Live your word by looking out.

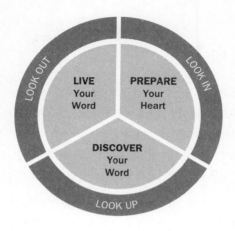

LOOK IN, LOOK UP, LOOK OUT

In the following sections, we walk you through these three steps to help you find your word or, perhaps better stated, to allow your word to find you. We're confident that there's a word meant just for you and when you live your word, it will have a profound impact on every area of your life.

One Word isn't only for the select few who are highly motivated. In fact, it works best for those who are tired of the same old thing and maybe even a little frustrated by previous failures.

One Word for One Year for One Life.

Truthfully, there is only one thing you need to do to put *One Word* into practice—if you're breathing, you qualify! You must have a desire to live life to the fullest and become the best you. If that's you, then *One Word* is for you.

There is no secret recipe. No hidden tricks. We're talking about *One Word* for One Year for One Life. That's it. Everyone has the skill and ability to do that. We know you can do it, because we've witnessed people from all walks of life and in every stage of life experience the power of *One Word*.

One Word Works

One Word is contagious. We've shared this powerful process with thousands of people who immediately put it into practice, and the results are always the same: unstoppable life change. You'll be amazed by your success and transformation—even in areas you've given up on—when narrowing your focus and simplifying your approach.

The *One Word* Process is something you can do with your team at work and your family at home, too. Just imagine if everyone in your workplace knew their word and lived it each day, thus making themselves and their teams better. Imagine how energizing this would be for your family as well.

One Word is timeless and powerful. It doesn't change with changing times or culture. It is built on the power of process . . . just three simple steps.

The process takes a little time, but the results are worth it. It doesn't matter whether you are a parent or a child, a senior or an adolescent, a business leader or a teacher, this process works!

Let's get started with the first step of the *One Word* process.

prepare your heart: Look In

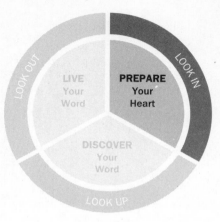

LOOK IN

John Wooden, one of the greatest coaches ever, led the UCLA basketball team to 13 national championships. He was the only person inducted into the Hall of Fame as both a player and coach. He would always tell his players, "Failing to prepare is preparing to fail." For him, preparation was a key ingredient to success.

When we talk about preparing your heart, we mean getting your heart ready by looking in. That takes preparation and, as Coach Wooden discovered, it's our first step to success in the *One Word* process. Every year, we are intentional about stopping and preparing our hearts. If you skip this step or rush through it, you are likely to miss out on the most rewarding and revealing part of the *One Word* journey. Preparing your heart creates fertile ground for life change.

Failing to prepare = preparing to fail.

Abraham Lincoln said, "If I had eight hours to chop down a tree, I'd spend six hours sharpening my ax." Nothing is more frustrating than chopping wood with a blunt blade, and nothing is more frustrating than going through life without focus. Taking the time to sharpen the ax makes the task successful. Most of us fail in the preparation, not in the task itself.

The Silent Killer

There's no question that it's hard to break away from the busyness of life. It has become the silent killer of our day. In the Chinese language, the word *busyness* is represented by single pictograph of two characters: *heart* and *killing*!

Busyness is a disease that's robbing us of life. It brings on stress and exhaustion, and it weights our hearts with anxiety so that we become numb and calloused to the most important things in life. Busyness throws us into survival mode and leaves no time for mission and meaning.

It has been said that busyness makes us stop caring about the things we care about. Some of us are addicted to busyness. When the alarm goes off, we hit the ground running. We are constantly on the go.

Activity does not mean achievement.

But if you're running the rat race, you're in the wrong race. As experts at multitasking, we've bought into the lie that *activity means achievement.* If you are like us, you may even feel guilty when you're not doing something, as though you should be filling up your time every moment. If we take a break, it's almost never in silence; we find something else to create noise and fill the void.

Make the Investment

The first and most important step of the *One Word* process is to *prepare your heart.* It means we need to escape from the busyness of life and take time to get our hearts ready by looking inward. The truth is, what you sow, you will reap. What you invest into this process, you will receive in return. The seeds you plant today will create the harvest you will enjoy tomorrow.

Sometimes, our hearts are similar to hard-packed soil, and the seed never takes root. Other times, it takes root and grows, but the worries, desires, and distractions of life choke it out. Then there are times when the seed falls on the good soil of a heart that is ready to receive it. That seed grows and produces a great harvest. If you want a great harvest, don't go through the motions: Prepare your heart. Take the time to look inward by opening your heart.

Right now, you might be wondering how much time is needed. We can't answer that for you, because it's different for each person. We know some individuals who begin to prepare their hearts to receive their word around Thanksgiving. That gives them a good four to five weeks before the New Year. They don't like to rush through it, so they enjoy the extended time to evaluate the possibilities. Others set aside one hour on December 31. Still others who read this book during the summer may want to take time to reflect and choose their word for the second half of the year. When the New Year approaches, simply choose another word for the year. Any approach works, but the path you choose depends on what you want to gain from this— simply a word or actual life change?

One Word is for any time of the year—it's never too late to start.

The most important thing is to detach from the business and stress of life to prepare. Whether it's April, August, or December, you will be ready for your word. Preparation paves the way for growth and harvest.

When it comes to preparing your heart and looking in, we follow two simple steps: (1) Unplug, and (2) Ask.

Unplug

Unplugging requires that we intentionally find solitude and silence. Being alone and quiet are tough disciplines for most of us. Unplugging doesn't come naturally and can feel awkward. We're much more comfortable with the TV on in the background or headphones in our ears. We like noise, because it keeps us company, but it will keep us from discovering our *One Word*.

When developing our *One Word* for the year, it's imperative to completely unplug from all distractions and create an environment conducive to silence. That means:

· No TV
· No music
· No computer
· No phone
· No other people
· No to-do lists

As you prepare your heart for discovering your *One Word*, it's challenging to find a place with no distractions or interruptions. We've found that getting up early, when it's still dark and before the family gets into full swing, is key. Others capitalize on the late-night hours. Sometimes, finding an isolated place in nature is helpful. Wherever you decide to go, create the environment to look inward and to discover what you need to quiet your mind and really listen to your heart.

Ironically, the first thing you'll experience in the silence is the unrelenting noise in your head. It's difficult to shut off the concerns of the day, your schedule, and the endless to-do lists waiting for you. It's an all-out battle to break through the noise of life.

Out of silence comes power.

But if you move past the initial awkwardness of silence and look inward, you'll be rewarded with clarity. You'll begin to see things more clearly and be refreshed by the renewing of your body, mind, and spirit. You'll begin to experience and enjoy a peace that you probably didn't think was possible.

When this happens, you will find it easy to discover your *One Word*. It has been said, "A word with power is a word that comes out of silence." Your word will be birthed out of solitude. Commit to unplugging.

Ask

While you're unplugged, take the next step and ask the following three key questions to prepare your heart for your *One Word*.

1. *What do I need?* This isn't necessarily about what we want, but what we truly need. What areas of our life need the most change, and why? This question helps to uncover some obvious and hidden issues that need your attention. It also jump-starts the list of possible words for the year.

2. *What's in my way?* Looking for obstacles or things that are preventing personal growth is a powerful process. "What is preventing me

from having what I need?" The answers to this question can be revealing. Sometimes the barriers are simply in our mind.

3. *What needs to go?* Sometimes, we are held hostage by past mistakes or pain. Bitterness and lack of forgiveness hold us back. Other times, the words *should have* or *could have* prevent us from moving forward. This question helps us identify the things we need to let go of in order to make progress.

These three questions are so powerful because they'll help you find a word that has true meaning in your life. Too often, we focus so much time on getting our *One Word* that we miss the real power—the *why* behind the word. When you know the why behind your word, you'll have greater power to live and share it.

The *why* is always more important than the *what*.

Discovering the *why* happens when we look at the past, the present, and the future. What are your past circumstances that you need to learn from? What is your current reality? Where do you want to go from here?

Situations and circumstances in the past happened for a reason—and *for us to reason*. They paint the picture of our life story. The answers to these questions help us understand where we are now and why we want to make improvements and changes.

Once you understand why you are drawn to a certain word, you create fertile ground for the word to be planted in your life.

discover your Word: Look Up

LOOK UP

Once you've prepared your heart, you are ready to receive your word. That's right, receive it. Contrary to what you might have thought, you don't have to chase after your word or feel stressed at the thought of trying to choose it. After you have prepared your heart, you're ready to simply look up to the Creator.

There is a word that's meant for each one of us—a word based on where we are in our lives and where God wants to guide us. That's why, in a room with hundreds of people, almost everyone will have a different word. There are different words for people with different circumstances and destinies.

The process of looking up is meant to be peaceful, not stressful. Filled with hope, not despair. Fueled by faith, not by fear. You don't have to force it or add it as another checkmark on your to-do list.

After preparing your heart, all you have to do is plug in and listen up. Then God will reveal your word to you.

Plug In

Plugging in requires that you make time for prayer. Whether you pray while taking a morning walk, going to bed, showering, gardening, or driving to work, prayer is simply having a conversation with God. When you express your needs and wants, struggles and failures, and hopes and dreams, you reveal your heart to God and allow God to share unconditional love for you.

Prayer should be our first response—not our last resort.

During your prayers, ask God to take control. This takes courage, because it pushes you out of your comfort zone. We prefer to be the *driver* of the car. We like to take control, roll up our sleeves, and get it done. But prayer takes some of the pressure off of us and places it in capable hands. You don't have to create your own word. God has a word for you.

While you are praying, ask God to reveal the word that is meant for you. Ask, "What do you want to do in me and through me?" After all, it's not about you picking a word that might be good for you. It's about *receiving* the word that is meant for you to live and share with others.

The *One Word* process is a journey to discover a "God word," not just a "good word." A good word is one that makes sense, because it is an area of your life that needs work or development. But a God word is more personal, and it's revealed to you specifically for this moment in time.

In the early years, the words we chose were 99 percent of our own choosing and only 1 percent God speaking. Even so, God still used the process! As we've become more experienced, we've learned to really listen and watch for God's lead in selecting the word. Now we can truly say, "It's not about us, but about God." We don't pick, God shows us.

Get a God word, not just a good word.

When we look up, we recognize that God knows what is best for us. A God word is best. Don't settle for anything less. Boldly ask God for the word; be open and willing to listen for that still, small voice, and wait for God to reveal your word to you.

Listen Up

The second part of looking up is to listen up. Most people talk to God, but few listen to God. After asking God to reveal your word, it's important to listen and be open to the word that God shares. God uses all means to communicate with us, and you never know when, where, and how your word will be revealed to you.

God may reveal your word while you are reading an inspirational book, a devotional, or the Bible. Some will hear their word while listening to a song. Others will hear a small voice that whispers their word to them. Some folks even receive their word in a dream. Many children have told us their words came to them while lying in bed or praying before bedtime. Others have said their word came while cooking or showering.

Jon received his word last year while hurting his knee jumping in the ocean. He heard the word *Surrender* and knew it was the word meant for him.

Jimmy hears most clearly from God when he's cycling or training. When working out, he listens to teaching podcasts and worship music. He writes down several words over time and asks God to confirm his word through scripture and by staying plugged in to the source.

Dan waits for his word with a Bible in one hand and his journal in the other. During this time, he reads, reflects, and writes down the thoughts and nuggets revealed to him. This allows him to look into God's Word for his *One Word*.

We can't tell you in what way your word will be revealed to you. But if you prepare your heart, ask God for the word that is meant for you, and listen for God to speak into your life, God will find the best way to share your word with you. When you look up, God gives you the eyes to see and the ears to hear the word you are meant to live this year.

balance
purpose
commitment
GOLOVE
opportunity
give ask
thankful
generous

live your Word: Look Out

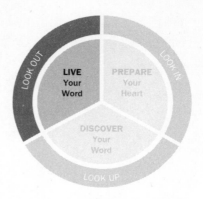

LOOK OUT

When your word comes to you, it may come in the form of a character trait, a discipline, a person, a spiritual focus, an attribute, or a value. The following examples of possible words are not meant to be a particular list from which to choose, but rather a starting point of ideas: *love, joy, patience, kindness, rest, prayer, health, train, flexible, devotion, intimacy, discipline, smile, commitment, overcomer, bold, positive, green, inspire, finish, purity, integrity,* and *strong.* Over the years, we have heard people share these and many other words that have special meaning to them. In fact, one of the things we love about sharing the *One Word* concept with others is hearing the fascinating words people choose and the reasons their word is meant for them.

But our favorite part about helping others find their *One Word* for the year is hearing how people have lived their word and the impact it had on their life.

Live It Out

Once you discover the word that is meant for you, then it's time to live it out. As the saying goes, this is where the rubber meets the road. This is the most important part of the process—your moment of truth!

This is the fun part. If you're like us, you're feeling a sense of excitement and anticipation. It's almost like the adrenaline rush before a big race or game. You've prepared your heart, discovered your word, and now it's time for life change! The process is exhilarating, but it will also prove to be challenging. You'll face obstacles you didn't anticipate. Most say that finding your word is the hardest part, but actually *living it* is. You will be stretched—we promise. But we often learn the most when we step out of our comfort zone, so stay the course. The results will be worth it.

The "Look Out" step has a double meaning: "Look out," and you'll begin to see opportunities all around you. "Look out," because *One Word* will change your life in unexpected ways.

Step outside your comfort zone.

You may immediately see some areas of opportunity in which you could improve. This is the low-hanging fruit. You may be tempted to think that this is going to be easy. Yet the difficult areas of life change are often revealed later. We have been amazed by how many unexpected lessons we've learned as the year unfolds.

It's essential to remember and focus on your word throughout the year. The stress and challenges of life will cause you to forget your word if you let them. We know this well through our own experience. If your word is not at the top of your mind, it will be forgotten.

Keep your *One Word* front and center.

Through years of trial and error, we've discovered simple and powerful ways to keep your *One Word* front and center throughout the year.

First, post your word in prominent places so you see it on a regular basis. What gets your attention gets your focus; what gets your focus gets done. The opposite is also true: Out of sight, out of mind. It is imperative that you regularly see your word.

It's *your* word, so own it, personalize it, and internalize it. Creating reminders is important. Here are some examples that have been very effective over the years:

- Write it down and post it in prominent places, such as your in kitchen, in your car, in your planner, or on your desk.
- Create a screen saver with your word.
- Paint your word on a sign and hang it where you will see it every day.

- Take a picture of your word and save it on your smartphone.
- Keep a journal and write down the insights and lessons learned each week.
- Start a *One Word* dinner discussion once a week where you talk about progress with your family.
- Create a weekly focal point or challenge every Monday. Choose one of the six dimensions of life.
- Post it in your locker at school.
- Look for sayings or quotes that relate to your word.
- Pick a song that reminds you of your word.
- Write a poem or prayer.
- Create a document on your computer to collect "All Things *One Word.*"
- Get a tattoo (we suggest a removable one).

The options to have fun with your word are endless. Enjoy the process. Find the ways that work best for you.

Second, share your word with your *Stretch Team*—that inner circle of friends and family most important to you and whom you trust without hesitation. We call it your Stretch Team because it consists of the people who stretch you and help you grow. Give them permission to ask you about your word. This keeps you accountable for staying on track. When you share with them how you are being shaped by your word, they will be inspired to join in the process as well.

A Few More Tips

As you progress in living out your *One Word* journey, we have a few tips. Some people try to approach *One Word* as they would New Year's resolutions. They see it as something to check off a to-do list; it either gets done or it doesn't.

But that's not how *One Word* works. Instead, you will probably experience your word as a journey of ups and downs that all help to shape you into the person you were created to be. You don't win or lose with *One Word*. Whatever you experience throughout the year, that's what is meant for you.

Don't check the box; experience the journey.

Once you have used a word, don't repeat it the following year. If you don't make the progress you think you should, or if you feel as though there is more to learn, that's okay. You may want to try the same word again, but resist the temptation for a do-over. You will never fully exhaust the meaning and application of your word. Let it stand as the year in which you learned lessons as a result of your word, even if you didn't fully master that word. If it is really tough living out your word, then that is part of your growth process. No recycled words. Each year is a brand-new word for a brand-new year.

No do-overs; opt for a new word each year.

When you do these two simple things—post your word prominently and share it with others—you ensure your growth. There will be no false starts or failures. You will experience highs and lows, but they are all part of the process. As you live out your word, let God use the simplicity of your *One Word* theme to revolutionize your everyday life.

balance
purpose
commitment
GO LOVE
opportunity
GIVE ask
thankful
generous

spread the **Word**

Imagine if we all lived out the word meant for us. Can you imagine what our families would be like? How about our workplaces, schools, and communities? How powerful would you be? How big of an impact would you have? If we could pull that off, we might just change the world!

Why not start spreading the word by taking your family through the *One Word* process? After experiencing the power of the process in 1999, Dan and Jimmy shared it with their wives and kids. Now they have a tradition of getting their

ONE WORD: A FAMILY EXPERIENCE

families together every New Year's Eve to paint their words on canvas tiles that they hang in the kitchen as a constant reminder. During this time, they even create *One Word* for the entire family that they focus on together.

Share the Power

In addition to your family, you can also spread the word to your school, work, sports team, church, or other organization to which you belong. For example, we have taken a number of school districts through the *One Word* process and have heard amazing stories. Some teachers post their words in the teachers' lounge so they can see their words each day and also help each other live their words. We also know of teachers who do this with their students and have their students make pictures of their words that they then post around the classroom.

We've also worked with a number of sports teams to help their coaches and players discover their words. Mark Richt, head football coach at the University of Georgia, had each player discover and share his word for the year. Players listed their words on big-screen televisions around the football facility to remind them to live their word.

Players for the Atlanta Falcons also came up with their words. Head coach Mike Smith's word was *Finish,* because he wanted himself and his team to finish strong in everything they did. He said it had a powerful impact on him and his team.

Hendrick BMW in Charlotte, North Carolina, featured a car in the middle of its showroom displaying the words chosen by each employee. Imagine all the employees coming into work every day and seeing their word and their coworkers' words on a car. Now imagine customers seeing these words, asking what they mean, and hearing how *One Word* helped Hendrick develop the best team and provide the best customer service possible. Talk about spreading the word!

The men at LifePoint Church in Finksburg, Maryland, discovered their words and shared them with each other to keep each other on track. The positive impact on marriages, families, and the local community has been remarkable. Many men told stories of marriages saved and relationships with children restored.

THE *ONE WORD* CAR

THE *ONE WORD* CAR (CLOSE UP)

ONE WORD HANDS

THE STAFF AT CHRIST'S CHURCH IN JACKSONVILLE, FLORIDA, WROTE
THEIR WORDS ON THEIR HANDS AND MADE A COLLAGE.

In addition to having each person in your family
and organization come up with his or her individ-
ual word, you can also come up with a *One Word*
focus for your entire organization.

For example, the entire executive leadership
team of the Fellowship of Christian Athletes, a
nonprofit organization that connects with more
than 2 million coaches and athletes, developed

a *One Word* theme for the year. The team's word, *Together,* became a unifying force for team members, as their commitment and loyalty to each other grew throughout the year. The word gave them a focus to center around and an awareness of staying together as they led the organization.

One Word makes others better.

When you spread the word to your family and organization, you not only make yourself better, you make everyone around you better. And when everyone in your organization chooses and lives their word, you become a more powerful and positive force in the world and make a greater impact. If you ever need help introducing the *One Word* concept to your organization, just let us know. It's our mission and passion to help others live their word.

balance
purpose
commitment
GO LOVE
opportunity
GIVE ask
thankful
generous

my
One Word

Every single time we have shared the con-cept of *One Word* with others, we get the same response: "I love it! I can't believe I've never done this before. It's so simple and obvi-ous. I can't wait to get started." And we get the same positive responses after participants have lived out their *One Word* for the year: "What a powerful year! I've learned so much. This is something I'll do for the rest of my life. By the way, my word for next year is . . ."

We have never heard this: "I tried that *One Word* thing and it didn't work." Not once! The only way it won't work is if you don't do it. It's never a question of whether *One Word* works. It's whether you will put *One Word* into action in your life. If you discover and live your word, it works every single time, because there is a word meant for you, and it is meant to change your life in a positive way.

To help you through the *One Word* process, we've created the following action plan to help you prepare your heart, discover your word, live your word, and spread the word.

Action Plan

Prepare Your Heart: Look In

Take a little time to:

1. Unplug from the noise.
2. Ask a few essential questions.

Get away from the noise and distractions of life, and create an environment to look inward, quiet your mind, and really listen to your heart. Then ask yourself these three questions, and write your insights here:

1. What do I need?

   _____
   _____
   _____
   _____
   _____

2. What's in my way?

   _____
   _____
   _____
   _____
   _____

3. What needs to go?

_____

_____

_____

_____

_____

Discover Your Word: Look Up

Now that your heart is ready, it's time to plug in and listen up.

Once you've prepared your heart, you are ready to receive your word. God has a word that is meant *for you*. Remember, God can use all means to communicate with us, and you never know when, where, and how your word will be revealed to you.

Ask God to reveal your word to you with this simple question: "What do you want to do in me and through me?" Write down what comes to your heart. Listen and be open to the word that God shares.

Once you discover your word, write it down in the space that follows.

my **One Word**:

_____

year:

_____

Download this page each year at GetOneWord.com

Live Your Word: Look Out

Once you discover the word that is meant for you, then it's time to live it out. Again, this is where the rubber meets the road.

Keep your *One Word* front and center. Write down three things you will do to make sure you have regular reminders of your word:

1. _____

2. _____

3. _____

Sharing your *One Word* with your Stretch Team ensures success. List three people in your inner circle with whom you'll share your word this week:

1. _____

2. _____

3. _____

Spread the Word

Share your excitement about your annual *One Word* with others! Tell them about your journey.

List three other organizations you think would love and benefit from this process, and tell them about it.

1. _____

2. _____

3. _____

You can visit www.GetOneWord.com to share a one-page overview of the *One Word* process with your family, team, or organization.

Congratulations! We are excited that you are now part of the *One Word* Team. We look forward to changing lives together . . . *One Word,* one person at a time. Let us know your word on our GetOneWord.com website.

GetOneWord.com

The power of *One Word* has already changed
thousands of lives. Now it's your turn. We have
produced free resources to help you do that.
These resources will help you put the *One Word*
process into practice.

- Share your story.
- Download *One Word* posters.
- Watch and submit *One Word* videos.
- Sign up for our free newsletter.
- Discover creative *One Word* reminders.

One Word That Will Change Your Team

If you are interested in taking your leadership team or organization through the *One Word* process, we conduct leadership retreats, training, and team-building sessions for all types of organizations. Following is our contact information.

E-mail: info@GetOneWord.com

Online: www.GetOneWord.com

Sign up for the free monthly newsletter:
www.GetOneWord.com

To purchase bulk copies of *One Word That Will Change Your Life* for large groups or your organization at a discount, please check with your favorite bookseller, or contact Wiley Special Sales at specialsales@wiley.com or (800) 762-2974.

Acknowledgments

There is an African proverb that goes, "If you want to go fast, go alone; but if you want to go far, go together." Writing a book is never a "go alone" journey. There are numerous people who we call our *One Word Dream Team*. We are so thankful for friends, family, and partners who have helped us live the *One Word* dream. Though we can't thank everyone, we would like to recognize the following people:

- The John Wiley & Sons, Inc. team. You believed in this project and inspired us to run with it. Special thanks to Matt Holt, Shannon Vargo, Elana Schulman, and Lauren Freestone. You are the best.
- Ramona "Touchdown" Tucker, you are one of a kind—always helping and serving in amazing ways. You are gifted!
- Dan Webster for helping us simplify our *One Word* process. You are a living example of authentic leadership.
- Our Heavenly Father, who not only gives us our *One Word*s each year but also abundant life

through the gift of Jesus. We are three men who are simply saved by grace and for that we are eternally grateful.

· Dan would like to thank his wife, Dawn, and children, Kallie, Abby, and Eli, for believing and loving at all times. Special thanks to Steve Fitzhugh for the challenge to discover his first *One Word* on the drive to Ocean City in 1999.

· Jimmy would like to thank his wife, Ivelisse, and their four amazing kids—Jimmy, Jacob, Johnny, and Gracie—for their constant encouragement, laughter, and love. You've made him the richest man on earth.

· Jon would like to thank his wife, Kathryn, and their two children, Jade and Cole, for their unyielding love and support. He would also like to thank Dan and Jimmy for sharing the *One Word* process with him and his family.

· All the *One Word* believers who have been using and spreading the concept for years.

About the Authors

Dan Britton serves as the Fellowship of Christian Athletes' Executive Vice President of International Ministry and Training at the National Support Center in Kansas City. He has been on the FCA staff since 1991, first serving for 13 years in Virginia and most recently as the Executive Vice President of International Ministry and Training. At St. Stephens High School in Virginia and later at the University of Delaware, Dan was a standout lacrosse player. He continued his career by playing professional indoor lacrosse for four years with the Baltimore Thunder, earning a spot on the All-Star team, and was nominated by his teammates for both the Service and Unsung Hero awards. He has coauthored two books, *WisdomWalks* and *WisdomWalks SPORTS*, and is the author and editor of nine FCA books. Dan is now a frequent speaker at schools, organizations, churches, conferences, camps, conventions, and retreats. He still plays and coaches lacrosse and enjoys running, and he has competed in the Boston

Marathon. He met his wife, Dawn, in an eighth-grade youth group. They currently reside in Overland Park, Kansas, with their three children: Kallie, Abby, and Elijah.

You can e-mail Dan at dan@fca.org.

Jimmy Page serves as a Vice President of Field Ministry and the National Director of the Health & Fitness ministry for the Fellowship of Christian Athletes. Growing up in the snow country of Rochester, New York, he became a three-sport athlete in high school and went on to graduate with two degrees from Virginia Tech. For nearly 20 years, he has been a leader in the health and fitness industry, operating wellness facilities affiliated with Sinai Hospital and Johns Hopkins. Jimmy is also a certified Nike Sports Performance Coach and hosts a radio program called *Fit Fridays,* blending spiritual, mental, and physical health principles that promote abundant life. He and his wife, Ivelisse, started a cancer foundation called believebig.org following her victory over cancer. Jimmy has coauthored three books, *WisdomWalks, WisdomWalks SPORTS,* and *PrayFit.* Jimmy is a frequent speaker at schools, churches, camps, and retreats, and he is a trainer for corporate, sports, and nonprofit organizations, challenging people to maximize their lives and make a difference. He has a contagious enthusiasm and passion for life. As a lifelong athlete, Jimmy enjoys coaching, cycling, and triathlons. Jimmy and Ivelisse were college sweethearts, and they reside in Maryland with their four children: Jimmy, Jacob, John, and Gracie.

You can e-mail Jimmy at jpage@fca.org.

Jon Gordon is a best-selling author and keynote speaker whose books and talks have inspired readers and audiences around the world. His principles have been put to the test by numerous NFL, NBA, and college coaches and teams, Fortune 500 companies, school districts, hospitals, and nonprofits. He is the author of *The Energy Bus Wall* (a *Wall Street Journal* best seller); *The No Complaining Rule; Training Camp; The Shark and the Goldfish; Soup: A Recipe to Nourish Your Team and Culture; The Positive Dog;*

and his latest, *The Seed: Finding Purpose and Happiness in Life and Work.* Jon and his tips have been featured on *The Today Show*, CNN, *Fox & Friends,* and in numerous magazines and newspapers. His clients include the Atlanta Falcons, Campbell Soup, Wells Fargo, State Farm, Novartis, and Bayer, among others. When he's not running through airports or speaking to businesses, hospitals, or school leaders, you can find him playing tennis or lacrosse with his wife and two high-energy children.

You can e-mail Jon at info@jongordon.com.